God's Warrior

The Life Story of Ray Prince

by Alta Tanis

Indian Life Books

Intertribal Christian Communications (Canada) Inc.
PO Box 3765 RPO Redwood Centre
Winnipeg, Manitoba R2W 3R6 Canada

GOD'S WARRIOR

Alta Tanis

Copyright © 1996 by
Alta Tanis

All rights reserved. No part of this book may be reproduced, transmitted, or transcribed, in any form or by any means, electronic or mechanical, including photocopying, recording, and storing in any retrieval system, except for brief quotations, without written permission from the publisher.

Unless otherwise marked, all Scripture quotations are from *The Holy Bible, New Life Version,* published by Christian Literature International, Canby, Oregon and are used by permission.

Cover art and design by Don Monkman

ISBN 0-920379-11-7

Printed in Canada

PREFACE

When we came to British Columbia in 1970, Ray Prince was a new Christian. Our paths often crossed for there were very few native Christians in B.C. at that time. We prayed for him as we learned of some of the struggles in his Christian life.

Ray is a storyteller. As I listened to some of his adventures and stories of the past, I realized that others would enjoy them too. When I approached him about writing some of them, he was willing to help me. He felt that it would be good to have this testimony of the way the Lord had led in his life.

Ray and Nellie were very patient and helpful as I probed, asked questions, many questions, and more questions. The past few years, we spent hours with the tape recorder going over the things Ray remembered from his life. Others were helpful, too. I gained insight from Lisette Hall's account of the Carrier people, as well as Bridget Moran's books. Richard Jules at the Kamloops Indian Band office helped me research about the treatment of Native soldiers when they returned from World War II. Many of the missionaries shared insights and memories.

I thank Tim Nielsen and Ed Hughes at Indian Life Ministries for their help and encouragement in putting this book together. Most of all, I thank my husband, Jess, for his constant encouragement and help. He gave me time to write, in our busy schedule, and even threatened to chain me to my desk until I finished this book!

This book was written to encourage the people in the native churches and fellowships across Canada and the United States. Ray's life is a picture of God's love and care. Ray doesn't deny his failures and he knows he is not perfect—but he knows the God who is! Ray is a prayer "warrior" and we pray that God's love through Jesus Christ and the power of the Holy Spirit will be shown in Ray's story.

—*Alta Tanis*

FORWARD

Finally, a book which pays tribute to one of Canada's First Nation members who rightfully owns the title "Warrior." Ray Prince is one of the well respected elders in the Native Christian community who served our country well during World War Two. Wounded twice, his courage, perseverance and commitment kept him fighting hard for the freedom and rights we and our children now enjoy.

God's Warrior takes you along on the journey of Ray Prince's life. You will be captured by this man's love for his family, his tradition, and his life on the trapline. You will also be filled with rage and emotion for what he encountered in the residential school. Hopefully you will gain a greater appreciation and understanding of the difficulties some have to face because of mistreatments in the past.

Also, God's Warrior presents a remarkable man who loves his family. You will also see the personal life, commitment and faith—a warrior's courage and commitment to the Lord Jesus Christ. The same courage Ray showed in his experience of fighting in the War is now shown in his service to the One Person Who means the most to him, the Lord Jesus Christ.

–Vincent Yellow Old Woman

Vincent Yellow Old Woman is an itinerant evangelist serving with NAIM Ministries. He is also board member of the Native Evangelical Fellowship of Canada (NEFC) and makes his home on the Blackfoot reserve at Siksika, Alberta.

CONTENTS

Chapter One
A warrior's tears 7

Chapter Two
Preparing for battle 12

Chapter Three
Battles and death 18

Chapter Four
Longing for home 22

Chapter Five
Running away 28

Chapter Six
A great escape 35

Chapter Seven
Alone in the bush 40

Chapter Eight
Victory in Europe 44

Chapter Nine
No longer an Indian 48

Chapter Ten
Searching for the truth 53

Chapter Eleven
Choosing life 58

Chapter Twelve
Growing in Christ 63

Chapter Thirteen
No fighting back 70

Chapter Fourteen
The power of forgiveness 76

Chapter Fifteen
A different battle 82

Chapter Sixteen
No fear of the future 87

DEDICATION

This book is dedicated to the memory of my grandfather, John Unger. He told me stories, read me stories, and shared with me his love of words and books. One of my earliest memories is the sound of his voice reading aloud on a winter day. He was an elder who told us the stories and the history of our family and inspired me to be a storyteller, too.

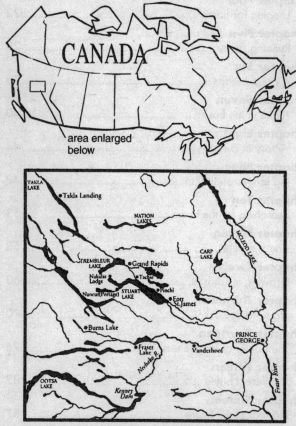

The land Ray Prince knows so well.

Chapter One

A warrior's tears

Ray didn't like the medicine smell or the sounds of wounded men in pain. It was Christmas Eve 1943, and Ray was in a hospital in Saint Andre, Italy. His chest hurt with every breath. The doctor said it was double pneumonia. His wounded leg throbbed, but he hoped he would heal quickly so he could return to his unit. He wanted to do his share with the other guys. The intense fighting in Italy during the Second World War seemed worlds away from Ray's home in western Canada.

Someone told him that his cousin, Herbert Prince, was wounded and was here in the same hospital. Ray wanted to see him but the nurse said Herbert's wounds were too serious and Ray was too sick. Later that night Herbert died. Ray felt so sad because he didn't get to see him and talk to his cousin one more time.

A whole week passed. The long days spent in the hospital seemed endless. In all his twenty years, Ray had never enjoyed staying still and quiet unless he was out in the bush hunting or fishing. On New Year's Eve, another boy he knew died of his wounds. Albert Jardine was from Stellakoh, British Columbia. He and Ray had gone to the residential school together when they were kids and now they served together in the Seaforth Highlanders. Ray felt an aching pain in his heart. Slowly, the tears trickled down his brown cheeks.

"You are crying," the nursing sister said.

"I am?" Ray felt he was caught doing something foolish, as he quickly wiped his eyes on his sleeve. "That boy, Albert, was my school mate."

"I tell you what," the nurse suggested. "You have a good cry and I will come back and bring you some cold water to drink."

The young nurse saw so many wounded men, and most of them were in much worse condition than this young Canadian boy with pneumonia blocking his breathing and shrapnel in his leg. His black hair and bronze skin told of his Indian heritage. His tear-filled brown eyes were full of pain.

When the nurse returned with the water, Ray had his tears under control. He felt a little better then. The patient nurse listened as he talked to her about the guys from his division who had died. His cousin Herbert. Now Albert. There were only a few Native boys from his home area of Canada in this terrible war. Now two of them had died in this army hospital in Italy.

During those days of recovery, Ray thought

longingly about his family that seemed so far away. He was only 16 when he left his home in northern British Columbia. He had been out in the bush, living in a log cabin on the trap line with his family, just as they did every year. He didn't talk to anyone about his plans but he made up his mind that when fall time came, he would join the army.

Ray didn't know much then about the rest of the world. His world was the Carrier Indian reserves near Fort St. James and the traditional trap line his family followed in northern B.C. He had attended a Roman Catholic residential school for about three years—but only until he ran away and went home. That school was at LeJac, near Vanderhoof, about 75 miles from his home in the mountains.

Ray's family sometimes heard news from the rest of the world on their small battery-powered radio. There were no newspapers where they were, even at their home in Fort St. James. There were no highways and hardly any roads—just a dirt trail leading into their village. The trail was more like a cow path with lots of mud holes. The only highway they ever heard about was the Caribou Highway that went south from Prince George to Vancouver. The rise to power of a man named Hitler, in far away Germany, did not matter much to Native people in that isolated area.

Ray remembered how he wanted to join the army for adventure. In the past few months he had found more adventure than he ever imagined. He recalled going into Fort St. James, one fall day in 1940 and asking a truck driver, "Could you give me a ride to Vanderhoof?"

"I'll give you a ride," the trucker replied. "If you will give me a hand loading this freight."

Ray helped the man load the truck, and was soon on his way. He knew the train went through Vanderhoof but he did not know the schedule. It didn't matter much to him which way he went. Whichever way the train went, Ray was going. Someone told him the train was leaving for Prince Rupert on the coast. It was a freight train and didn't have a passenger car, so Ray climbed on a flat car.

When the train stopped at Smithers, a train official asked, "What are you doing here?"

"I'm going to Prince Rupert to join the army," Ray told them.

"You can join the army right here," they told him.

"No, I'm going to join in Prince Rupert," Ray said. So they let him go on. It was evening when the train pulled into the coastal town.

In November, the climate on the coast was not as cold as Ray's home in the mountains, but it was raining. A cold, wet Indian boy walked around the small town of Prince Rupert all night. He knew it would cost too much money to go to the hotel.

The next day he met a girl who suggested he could get a job at the local salmon cannery. She took him home to her family so he could have some lunch with them and wash up. He was dirty with the soot from the train and very hungry. Her family was very good to Ray. They liked this handsome young Native boy with a twinkle in his dark brown eyes and they said he could stay with them.

A Chinese man at the cannery, hired him to

load salmon into a box car. Though the wages were low, Ray worked there for a few weeks before he joined the army.

Chapter Two

Preparing for battle

Ray joined the armed forces at Prince Rupert and on December 2, 1940, the government arranged for him to board a steamer to travel down the British Columbia coast to Vancouver. The rugged Pacific coast was a new experience for the boy from the bush. From the bustling city of Vancouver, the army sent the new recruits by train to Vernon, in the southern B.C. interior. From there they travelled through the Rocky Mountains and across the lonely prairies to Winnipeg, Manitoba.

Camp Shiloh near Brandon, Manitoba, was the camp where Ray had basic training. The officers soon learned that this native boy was an excellent shot—he didn't miss the target! The physical training did not seem hard to Ray, compared to the life he experienced every day at home on the trap line.

In February, 1941, the young men of the Seaforth Highlander battalion learned they were going overseas. In preparation, they had to go before a medical board for examination. Ray remembered clearly the examining physician, Major Sutherland.

Ray stood in front of him. "How old are you?" the major asked.

"Eighteen," Ray answered, adding a year to his age, to agree with what he had put on his papers.

The major examined him, looked at his teeth, and then told Ray, "I am a doctor. I know how old you are."

Ray's heart skipped a beat, but his brown eyes didn't blink. "I want to go with them boys," he said. "I trained with them and I'm used to them and I'm ready to go." Ray and the others had heard that Germany was bombing England every night. All the young men were eager to go and get involved in the war. Ray's heart raced with excitement when he thought of being a warrior and fighting the enemy. He didn't want to be kept behind in Canada.

The major didn't argue. He signed the papers and Ray was on his way to Halifax, Nova Scotia. They boarded a ship there, and a convoy of about 40 ships began the trip across the Atlantic Ocean.

Ray's company sailed on the ILE DE FRANCE, a big ship that was a French luxury liner in peace time. He found out some interesting things about these luxury liners. The cows used to be kept where he was bunked down. The "cow deck" was now converted into quarters for the armed forces! There had been chicken coops in there, too. Someone explained to him that there was no refrigeration so the ship carried cows and chickens for fresh milk and eggs when they were at sea with a passenger list of rich people. In pre-war days, when the liner put into port, it took on different animals to use. Commissioned for war purposes, it was still a beautiful ship. In spite of his accommodations, Ray enjoyed exploring every corner of it.

The trip across the north Atlantic took sixteen long days. It was bitter cold and the ship got so iced up that it was listing—tipping to one side! In the extreme cold it seemed everything froze at one time or another. It took a long time for things to thaw out.

Silent unseen German U-boats torpedoed some ships in the convoy during the dark nights. Ray didn't know how many ships and men were lost. It seemed that each morning they would wake up to realize there was an empty space where some ship had vanished. Their ship had to go slow and zig-zag. Every seven minutes it changed course. There was a great feeling of relief when they reached England safely in the ship that was almost coated with ice.

Ray remembered how, at home in Fort St. James, one native elder had come to him and prayed for him before he went into the army. Wassa Leon said to him, "No matter what you do, never forget God. Pray to Him when you need Him." Ray didn't know much about God but his parents had taught him to pray. He found many times that he needed to pray during his adventures in the war.

The army sent Ray to northern Scotland to train for amphibious landings. It was a tough training course for special forces and Ray stuck it out for the entire two years. Some guys did not make it all the way through the training period. Ray felt pleased that he was tough enough to complete the training!

Ray was also glad his father had taught him to listen to his elders. He knew he didn't have much education. Most of the fellows had much more schooling than he did. He made up his mind to listen carefully to all the lectures—and there were lots of lectures! He learned how to handle the equipment and the weapons. "That's how I learned," Ray said, "I learned by listening. I figured if I didn't listen, I would be left behind. It's just like a coach, you know, if you don't listen you'll miss the play, eh? In football, that is what happens. This is the way it is in the army, too."

Ray had learned, in the traditional native way, to listen to his parents and elders, and to obey. He tried hard to obey every order in the army.

His parents had also taught him never to believe in defeat and never give in to it. If you do, "you are embarrassing your ancestors," they told him. Ray remembered their advice when the lectures were long and the training was so tough and tiring that some of the other fellows dropped out.

The Atlantic coast near Inveraray, Scotland has the worst weather in the world, Ray was sure. The wind blew continually, things were never still and it was always wet. Big storms battered the great rock cliffs that rose from the sea. The temperature didn't get as cold as his home in British Columbia, but he did not like the constant rain. The dark clouds that hung over the rocky peaks made those two years of training go very slowly.

Ray had always been strong and healthy. After that rigorous training he felt he was ready to face any enemy. All the young men were restless and eager to get into the war and fight. Finally, early in 1943, they boarded a large troop ship. Hundreds of troops joined the ship in Liverpool, England but no one knew where they were going. Ray was on that same ship for 28 days. It was a tiresome, boring time—twenty-eight days of just waiting. The men exercised daily and saw a few old movies. Water was rationed. Drinking water became almost too warm to drink and they showered in salt water. Suddenly, without warning, orders came and they were on their way!

Ray's group joined with other ships in a huge convoy. Some of the ships were from the United States. Ray watched, his eyes wide in wonder, as the convoy sailed through the very narrow Strait of Gibraltar, just a few ships at a time, into the Mediterranean Sea. Ray and the other soldiers received Greek translation books, so they assumed they were going to invade Greece. They struggled with the pronunciation of the strange Greek words for days. It was nothing like the soft, familiar sounds of Ray's native Carrier language.

The ships put into port at Algiers in North Africa. The troops changed to smaller ships—invasion ships! At sea again, the men received new uniforms with short pants to wear. Ray felt foolish. No Indian man that he knew ever wore short pants! But he didn't argue.

The Greek language books were thrown away to be replaced with instruction books in the Italian language. The army wanted to be sure they would know the difference between the Italian language and German language when they heard it spoken. The German forces were now occupying Italy. Ray and his fellow soldiers were going to land in Italy, on the island of Sicily—not in Greece. Ray's amphibious patrol would go in first to check things out and his unit would take the first wave of attack.

Chapter Three

Battles and death

Excited and tense, the young soldiers crammed into the rubber raft felt their stomachs churn with anticipation. The raft tossed on the waves of a stormy sea as it edged towards shore. This was very different from the cold, wet days of training for the last two years in Scotland. Here, off the coast of the island of Sicily, it was a hot, stormy night. It was eleven p.m. on July 9, 1943. In three hours the main Canadian invasion of Sicily would begin on "Sugar" Beach.

Ray and the others in his patrol came onto the beach quietly in their soft-soled shoes. Each man was armed with hand grenades and a tommy gun. It was hard climbing, but the soldiers had trained for this. They soon scaled the high, jagged cliff, undetected in their camouflage uniforms.

Carefully working their way close to the German placement they found a unit of German soldiers, just as they expected. The hours spent studying the Italian language in their little books was useful now. The conversation they heard was not Italian! Ray was about ten feet away from a German soldier. He recognized the distinctive shape of his helmet. Then he quietly slipped back to report to the officer in charge.

"How many troops?" The officer asked, "Did you see their guns?"

"There are lots of troops and lots of guns. I am sure they know we are coming in, from the way they are pointing out there. They sure are excited," Ray told him. "They're moving around a lot."

"That's good," the officer replied. "Now we know where they are."

Canadian invasion troops, alongside the British Eighth Army, landed on "Sugar" Beach about two in the morning, July 10, 1943. "Here we go," Ray's officer whispered as he shot the green flares toward the ships that were waiting. These flares signalled that everything was okay and ready to go.

The German defensive barrage began as the ships started coming in to "Sugar" Beach. Destroyers and landing craft came right to the beach, within about 400 yards. They dashed in at full speed and then they reversed. Tucked into the jagged cliffs, with the bullets flying just over their heads, Ray and his patrol were in the war, at last. The fierce battle lasted all day. Finally, the Allies won control of the area.

This landing in Sicily was eleven months before the famous D-Day landing and battle at Normandy in France. It took the Allied forces thirty-nine days to take Sicily. Ray's regiment, the Seaforth Highlanders, First Division, fought bravely and well.

Around the first of September, the Allied army hit the mainland of Italy. From the toe of Italy, they drove north. Ray remembers the towns and the battles of the two years he spent fighting in Italy. Reggio, in the toe of Italy's boot. Foggia. Campobasso. Potenza. Ortona. These were some places the Allied troops battled through.

It was a painfully slow struggle as the Allied forces fought the German army in Italy and ended the career of the Fascist dictator, Mussolini. The brutal battles against the Nazi forces involved 93,000 Canadian soldiers. Over 5000 died and 20,000 were wounded. They faced floods, mud, mountains and the winter cold. The ash that was "fallout" from the volcano, Mount Vesuvius, made the snow mushy, gray, and dirty. It was hard to walk through it and not at all like the crunchy, cold, white snow of northern British Columbia.

Ray could handle the cold better than the men from warmer climates. "They talk about sunny Italy," Ray observed. "Sometimes there was six inches of snow on the ground. I ran or walked most of the time. Back and forth—sometimes we would lose ground. It wasn't all rosy."

It is difficult for Ray to talk about the actual shooting in the war. The first time he started shooting at people it was very hard, but most of the time he didn't know who he was shooting at. At night, he heard a noise and he shot there. It bothered him but he obeyed orders.

At Christmas time in 1944, Ray was on the

front line. Many wounded were on the field before him and Ray saw one German soldier move slightly. He didn't know why he did it but, during a lull in the fighting, he went out to the young soldier. Raising the wounded man up, Ray held him and hugged him a bit. Wordlessly, the young man pointed to his chest. Ray reached into the pocket of the German soldier's uniform and took out a small picture in a folder. It must have been a picture of his wife and baby that Ray held for him to see. Tears rolled down the young soldier's face. Ray knew the boy was dying and it really hit him hard in his heart. Ray cried, too, and held him in his arms until life was gone.

"You cannot do that. It's against regulations," the officer in charge scolded. But Ray was glad he had reached out to the dying man.

Ray was inside the lines and both sides had suffered many losses. From that day on, the face of the dying soldier often came to Ray's mind. The war got harder. He longed to be back in Canada, but home seemed very far away.

Chapter Four

Longing for home

All through his time of military service, Ray often thought of his mother and dad at home in British Columbia. He thought that they were different from some of the other Indian families. Ray remembered that sometimes at Christmas his mother would sit the children down on the floor of the cabin at Inzana Lake and tell them about Jesus. He did not remember how young he was when he first heard about the birth of the Christ child but he remembered about the star and the wise men. Years later, he and his brother, Fred, wondered about this.

"How did she know?" Fred asked. "Our mother never went to school and didn't know how to speak English."

"The priest didn't speak our language," Ray said, "She didn't learn it from the priest. I think the Spirit of God taught her."

Ray's father was different, too. He would pray when he was out in the bush. He would tell the children, "You pray to God. Nobody else will help you in this world, just God."

"How about those priests?" Ray once asked.

"Some of them are all right," was the reply. "Some of them are Christians, but some of them are not Christians at all." Ray was sure his dad knew the difference.

The Roman Catholic priests had come into northern British Columbia many years ago, in the 1840's. Most of the Indian people went to the Roman Catholic church at Fort St. James. The church made very strict rules and required obedience from the Native people. The early priests punished those who didn't obey.

"We were always left behind in the Catholic Church. The white people used to be up in the balcony—that was their place to worship—no Indians were allowed up there. We had to sit down on the floor of the church. No bench, we had nothing to sit on," Ray recalled in later years. "We minded that."

Ray knew his dad didn't lie and he never heard him swear in all his life. His parents taught their children to be honest, to be responsible, and to pray every morning, and thank God for their food. Ray's dad, Alec Prince, grew up at Fort St. James but did not live on the Indian reserve. He and his brother Jean-Marie, had been sent south to the St. Joseph's residential school near Williams Lake for a few years. It was a long trip by barge on the Fraser River as far as Soda Creek, and then inland to Williams Lake.

Alec's father, Joe Prince, was called "dayi cho" in the Carrier language, which meant "big chief." Ray's grandfather and other Carrier people cleared the land for the Roman Catholic mission that was established at Fort St. James in the 1870's. They worked hard clearing the land, building a log church and homes for the priests and themselves.

Ray's mother, Rosalie Austin, was from "K'uz che", the Grand Rapids reserve. To reach Grand Rapids you travelled 46 miles along the north shore of Stuart Lake and then 12 miles north on the Tachie River. Rosalie didn't go to school and her parents had never gone to school either. They only spoke the soft Carrier language.

His parents, Alec and Rosalie, married in 1913. When Ray was born at Grand Rapids in August 1923, he joined the family of four brothers and two sisters.

Ray's dad was a very quiet, shy man. Yet, when he spoke, Ray soon learned to obey him. Ray respected his father. It was a hard life but other Native families in the area lived in the same way. They lived off the land and the children had to learn what they needed to know to survive.

The Prince family had a team of horses and a cow. There were about seven white families in Fort St. James when Ray was a boy. Often Ray's dad would provide them with wood or milk, and sometimes meat. Occasionally, he guided fishermen on the lake in the summer.

The family moved out onto the trap line around the first of October each fall and stayed out there most of the winter. Ray's dad came into town to get some groceries that they might need in mid-winter. In spring, they usually brought in many furs of the marten, lynx, mink, and fox.

The family was comfortable in the warm log house. Among the things she taught them, Ray's mother insisted they keep themselves clean. Even out on the trapline, the kids had to heat water and bathe in the round tub they used at the cabin. It was the same when they were in town.

Ray was the youngest in the family but that didn't mean he was allowed to get by without working. His parents were strict, and they worked hard. They wanted their children to learn to be like that too.

"They loved us very much," Ray fondly remembers. "We were always aware that they wanted to teach us their ways. 'This is the way,' they used to tell us."

Ray never remembered ever getting up in the morning before his mother. When he got up, even if it was four or five in the morning, she was already doing something—maybe sewing or beading, or making bannock. He could see her dark head bent over her work in the lamplight.

Ray's mother was just a bit over five feet tall, but she was strong. Ray thought she was like the superintendent of the family. She made up the schedule for the whole year and planned all the things they must do. She marked the time to go hunting in the fall, the time to go trapping in the winter and, in springtime, the time to plant the garden. After planting, the family seemed to relax for a little while before cutting and stacking swamp hay for the horses.

After haying, they went fishing and prepared the dried fish for next winter's food for the sled dogs. Then they went hunting and dried moose meat and venison for the family's winter food supply.

The family used dog teams for transportation. There were no snowmobiles like the people used in later years. There were no motors or electricity. Everything was hard work. The first modern thing Ray's family owned was a gasoline light. They pumped air into it, like a camping lantern, and lit it with a match. The family could hardly believe how bright it shone through the whole cabin. "Gee," Ray said, "It was really bright."

For years after that, Ray still sensed when it was the right time to go hunting, go trapping, go fishing, or do the haying. He didn't always do those things, but the rhythm of the seasons with his parents was always a part of him.

Ray always enjoyed the times he spent with his grandparents, too. He respected his mother's dad, Austin Williams, a big man over six feet tall. He was a hard worker and set a good example for his children and grandchildren. He would skid logs with a team of horses and build barns and buildings for people. He had a big garden each summer, and sold strawberries and other produce to the white people. He always had a big grocery box filled with canned stuff and staples like sugar and flour. Ray admired how he was always thinking ahead and working hard to provide for the family.

Ray's sister, just older than him, was Matilda. She died when she was about ten years old. Once Ray's dad said, "I made a big mistake in my life."

"Why do you talk like that?" Ray's mother asked.

"I made a bad mistake. I loved that little girl so much, it was like I forgot God," he said. "God took that little girl from me."

Ray knew his father was really sorry for that and felt sad about it. He didn't know for sure if that's what really happened. He thought his dad must believe in a very jealous God.

Ray had a happy childhood learning from his parents and grandparents. He especially enjoyed life in the bush, out on the trapline.

One of their neighbours, in Fort St. James, was a couple from Hamburg, Germany. Ray had known them all his life. Ed Cozy and his wife liked the Native people and taught them to make sauerkraut and gave them help with gardening. Ray sometimes helped Ed with his pack horses. Ed taught him how to shoe horses and how to pack them. He taught some Indian people how the Germans made beer. When Ray's mother was sick, Amy Cozy brought soup and cared for her and the family. Ray played with the three Cozy boys and got along with them really well. They were good people and he felt comfortable with them. He never imagined that someday he would be fighting against the German people in Europe.

When Ray was about seven the day came when his parents decided he should go to school. The Catholic priests had a residential school on the shore of Fraser Lake. Ray's brothers and sister attended there and Ray was sent away to be educated by the nuns and priest at Lejac Indian School.

Chapter Five

Running away

Quietly, before anyone was awake, Ray sneaked into the school kitchen and took a piece of ham and some bread. Slipping them into his pockets, he carefully opened the door. As it closed behind him, the ten-year-old boy felt he was finally free. He took a deep breath of the crisp morning air and headed for the small town of Fort Fraser. He knew it was a long way from Lejac Indian school to where he was headed. As he ran away from the residential school that cold November morning he was glad to be going home. He decided to follow along the railroad tracks so he walked on the ties.

Ray soon came to the river. The only way across was the high railroad bridge. When he was about halfway across the trestle he heard the rumbling sound of the freight train coming. The old railroad bridge did not have guard rails and it was too far to get to either side of the river. He didn't know how soon the train would be there or what to do! He was afraid to lie down between the tracks and let the train pass over him. He swung down by holding tightly onto the ends of the rough wooden ties. He hung suspended high over the deep river from that wooden trestle, while the train thundered over above him.

The heavy train vibrated and rattled the ties and shook him violently. He was afraid that any minute he would lose his grip and fall into the rushing, cold Nechako River below him. It seemed to take a long time for the train to cross but he held on desperately and he made it. His arms ached and felt so weak he could hardly pull himself back up onto the tracks!

Ray stayed with an old man in Fort Fraser that night. He didn't tell him he was running away from school but he guessed the man probably knew what he was doing. The old man didn't ask Ray any questions. About four the next morning, before the man was awake, Ray woke up and left his cabin.

That day Ray walked a long way—all the way to Vanderhoof. Most of the time he walked on the railroad ties. He didn't want to leave tracks in the snow that could be followed. Sometimes he went off to the side but he followed the tracks, not the road where he thought they might be looking for him.

Ray had been in school at Lejac Indian school, close to Fraser Lake, since 1930 when he was s< years old. He ran away after about three years and never went back.

Ray thought the school was a really terrible place to live. It was like forced labour and some children were very small. When the kids went out in the cold, bringing in wood or working outside, they used old socks to wrap around their hands. The sisters didn't give them any mitts and sometimes no socks. Some were just wearing rubber gum boots on bare feet and they were freezing! It was really a hard life. Like the other children, Ray missed his parents and his home.

During most of the day, Ray was very sleepy because the boys had to get up early in the morning and do a lot of hard work. They went straight to the barn, cleaned up with some snow, shovelled out the manure and did all their chores. The boys worked in the barn and did the gardening. There was always work to do. The sisters never gave them a hot drink in the morning. Sometimes, though, they sneaked a drink of warm milk from the cows when they were milking them in the barn.

The girls did all the laundry, sweeping, dusting, and dishwashing. They were taught knitting, crocheting, basic sewing and mending.

At the Lejac school there was not much time in the classroom. About all Ray learned was how to talk English and how to read and write it a little. All his life, he had spoken the Carrier Indian language and had never needed to learn English. The children were taught Catechism and learned all about the Roman Catholic Church. This seemed to be considered more important than everything else.

"I also was taught to give to the church," Ray said, "To sacrifice even a nickel if I had it. They taught me to kneel down and pray, but they didn't teach me to pray to Jesus Christ. The only time I prayed was when I was in trouble and needed help. I never saw a Bible. I didn't know what it said."

The priest and nuns often beat the children for breaking very minor rules. For punishment, the priest often hit the palms of a child's hands with a large dried willow switch. After each stroke they waited for the child to cry. Most of the kids would stand rigid without flinching. The blows were hard. They stung and hurt and resulted in swollen hands.

One thing that brought immediate punishment was speaking in Carrier. Speaking their Indian language was against the rules. It seemed that the school staff tried to make the Indian children ashamed of their language and their culture.

Another thing puzzled Ray—they couldn't even talk to their sisters. They were not to even look at any of the girls. Punishment for breaking any rules was strict. The children were often whipped or made to kneel down with arms stretched out for a long time until their arms just ached!

Ray's brothers and sister went to the same school. The Native girls had pretty, long hair. It had to be cut off right up to their ears. Ray thought they looked awful. He knew the girls also felt bad about it. Some said they felt that they looked like clowns.

Today, Ray asks, "I wonder how in the world they could be so cruel. Yet they believed in God and they were educated people. If there were just one good, tenderhearted nun or priest, it would have made all the difference, but I never met any. We were always under surveillance. They were always watching us. If the kids laughed or giggled, they got a good licking. There was no freedom. Everything you did, there was someone in charge of you—

no freedom."

The food was terrible, too. Once they bought some whitefish from the local Indians near the school. The fish was already spoiled before they served it to the kids. The sister who was cooking just threw it in the pot and boiled it—guts and all! She cooked it like that and that is what they had to eat. It was so terrible it made Ray feel sick. He wanted to go home.

The priest and nuns ate very well. They even had waitresses to serve them. They enjoyed delicious-smelling meals like roast beef, or ham with pineapple. They also had tasty desserts. The children in the dining room right next door ate mostly beans and porridge. Sometimes the milk was sour, if there was milk at all for the porridge. If the children had meat it was boiled until it was tasteless. Eventually, Ray came to believe that the Indian department was in cahoots with the priests at the Lejac school. Don't educate those Indians!

Five boys ran away from the Lejac school one winter in the thirties. They tried to walk home to Fort Fraser across the frozen lake. It started snowing heavily and became a blizzard. The search party found their frozen bodies huddled together, trying to keep warm as they died.

Ray made up his mind to run away—he decided he just had to go. He didn't tell anyone that he was leaving—not even his brothers.

By the time Ray got to Vanderhoof, it was early evening. He saw two men standing on the road by the bridge and he sneaked right up behind them through the bush. He stayed hidden quietly because one was a Royal Canadian Mounted Police (RCMP) officer and the other one was a priest. He knew the priest and he was sure they were watching for him. Ray guessed the white people would leave for supper so he stayed there, shivering in his fear and excitement. Afraid to move, he chewed on a bit of the ham from his pocket. It seemed like hours, as he waited for them to leave. He would have to cross that bridge. That was the only way that led north to Fort St. James.

"We'll go eat and then we'll come back." Ray heard them say as they got into their car. They were going down the road when Ray ran across the river bridge. He guessed the car didn't have a rear view mirror—they never looked back.

He crossed that river and went across country to a ranch where an old man they called Charlie lived. He was a trapper and he had dogs, and dogs, and more dogs. It was a real dirty place but he let Ray stay overnight with him. He was an ex-RCMP and he asked questions. "What are you doin' here?"

"Oh, just looking around," Ray said. "I'm looking for a horse."

Ray really would have liked to find a horse that he could ride back to Fort St. James. He was a good rider, but he didn't find a horse. Anyway, he stayed at Charlie's place that night. The next morning Charlie cooked some mush and it was just like Lejac Indian School—no sugar or milk! Ray choked down some of it and hit the road again.

Ray had just a little piece of the ham left in his pocket and a little sharp stick. He didn't know why he had that sharp stick but he chewed on the ham as he trudged along. His shoes crunched on the hard-packed snow. He walked just off the side of the road, running most of the time to keep warm. If he heard anyone coming along the road, he hid in the bushes. He wanted to get as far away from Lejac Indian School as he could. He didn't know what his mother and dad would say when they saw him.

Walking all day, the runaway boy got to Fort St. James that same evening. He had come about seventy-five miles from Lejac Indian school in three days and he felt tired and hungry.

Ray's Aunt Julie lived right on the Stuart River, on the way to Fort St. James. He went there first. His aunt could see that he was very hungry. She gave him bread and jam and tea. Ray really liked that. He ate quickly while she talked to him in the warm kitchen.

"Your mom and dad are probably out on the trap line," she told him. "There's nobody around town."

Ray stayed with her a little while and then walked on toward his dad and mother's house in the village. Sure enough, everything was locked up tight and no one was around.

Chapter Six

A great escape

Ray sat on a big rock near the government wharf on Stuart Lake at Fort St. James. It was warm in the sun on this late fall day. Ray knew the lake would soon be starting to freeze a little. There were just a few cars in the country in those days, but all the native people had boats and outboard motors. About four o'clock, Ray heard the familiar sound of an outboard motor coming down the lake. The boat landed right at the government wharf below where he was sitting. It was Damien Pierre from Tachie.

Ray ran down to the boat and asked, "Are you going back?"

"Yeah," he said, "I'm in a hurry cause that lake is going to freeze. I got to pick up the Indian agent and the Indian police and a doctor. I'm going to bring them back to Tachie."

"Well, I want to go up there, too," Ray told him.

"Your mother is farther up at Grand Rapids," Damien replied. "That's where they are. Maybe your grandfather is still at Tachie. You can ride up there with me tonight."

"Sure," Ray said, "But I run away from school and they are looking for me."

"Oh, I'll just cover you up in the back," Damien grinned. He handed Ray some old-fashioned hardtack, (a dry hard biscuit), and covered him with a big tarp.

The men going to Tachie sat up in the front of the boat when the officials came. The river boat was long and Damien had covered Ray completely with the tarp. Lying under it, he ate that dry hardtack on the forty-six mile ride up the lake and the officials never knew he was there.

An old Polish man had a store at Tachie. The passengers got off there and went to the village and Ray quickly got out of sight! He thought it was funny that the people looking for him paid for the boat ride that took him home.

As Damien said, his grandfather was still at Tachie. So Ray got a ride with him and he told his grandfather the truth.

"I ran away from school. I don't like it. The food is no good," Ray said. "I'm more happy on the trap line."

"I don't know what your mother will say, " his grandfather said, shaking his head. He knew Ray's mother wanted her children to stay in school and learn. She would not approve of this. Ray was quieter than usual as he rode in the boat with them the twelve miles on the river from Tachie to Grand Rapids.

At Grand Rapids, Ray went home to his mother. She was glad to see him but she didn't agree with him that he should have run away from school. She didn't like it at all. Her dark eyes were troubled, but she didn't say much about it.

That evening Ray went to visit his uncle. William's wife was a sister of Ray's mother. Ray saw all their stuff sitting there, packed up and ready to go out in the bush. He thought he knew where they were going.

"You ready to go out to the trap line?" Ray asked.

"Yeah," he said, "I'm going to go in the morning." His brother, Frank, was going out too.

"So which way you going?"

"Oh, I'm going up to Kazchek," he said.

Ray said, "Is it okay if I go with you?"

"Sure, you can come with us," his uncle said.

Ray's intention was to travel part of the way with them and then he was going to go across country to his dad. So that evening he arranged to go with his uncle but he didn't tell anyone his real plans.

"I'm going with William out on the trap line," Ray told his mother.

"Oh, that's good," she said. "That's good. You go with him." She gave him a warm blanket and new moccasins and she got ready everything that he would need. His mother always did that. She prepared the men for trapping with a packsack of food and all they needed. That was the custom of the Carrier women. The next morning Ray went with the men.

There was a junction on the way to Kazchek—one trail goes to Kazchek Lake and the other goes to Inzana Lake. They called it Timberfold camp. Ray picked up his stuff and was just going to head for Inzana Lake.

"Where are you going?" William said.

"I'm going to Inzana Lake."

"You can't go there, you got to go with us," he said. "There could be grizzlies around here and it's getting dark."

"It doesn't matter," Ray said, "I'm okay," and he left. His uncle shrugged. He knew Ray was an independent boy and he thought Ray could take care of himself.

Ray didn't mind being alone. His people had always lived here and this was where he belonged. His grandfather, and his ancestors before him, had trapped these lakes and rivers for 500 years or more. He was happy to be back here in his own country. Ray felt at home here. He felt free. It was about six miles to their cabin at the end of the lake and he knew that trail along the lake very well.

When he got to the cabin, Ray saw that no one was there. His dad and brothers, Walter and Teddy, probably went farther north to another lake to check traps. Ray was at the cabin alone for four days before his dad and brothers came back. He kept busy cutting firewood, and checking the traps in the area.

When he returned, Ray's dad wanted to know, "What are you doing here?"

Ray hurriedly told him, "I run away from school. I didn't like that school."

"What did your mother say?"

"She didn't like it. She said I never should have run away," Ray said. "I didn't like that place cause the food was terrible and it was just not right for me to be there. I would rather be up here. I don't learn anyway. I'm always feeding cows, or feeding pigs, or working on the farm there. I'm not getting to learn what I want."

His dad didn't say anything more about it. They stayed there until Christmas, when they went back down to Fort St. James.

Chapter Seven

Alone in the bush

Ray hurried across the frozen swamp toward the inviting light in the window of the warm cabin. Surely his uncle Jean-Marie Prince must be back by now, fixing himself some food. Ray had been out on the trapline, setting traps, most of the day. When he had left in the morning, he had taken the short-cut across the frozen swamp. Now he was coming back on the same trail. Thinking about how hungry he was, Ray forgot his dad's warning that the ice on the swamp could be thin and dangerous this early in the fall.

Ray's dog, "Weasel," was with him, following a rabbit track through the low bushes. "Weasel" was as white as a real weasel, except for a little black smudge right on his tail. In the Carrier language his name was "Nohbai."

Suddenly, the thin ice gave way over a deep hole and Ray plunged into the cold, dark swamp water. The water was over his head. He came up gasping. There was nothing he could grab, nothing he could reach, and no way to hang onto the sides. He couldn't get out! His coat and boots were pulling him down into the freezing water. Ray knew he wouldn't last long as he struggled to keep his head above the water.

Then he saw his dog, Weasel, inching out onto the ice with his head down on the ice. Ray grabbed his ears and the dog pulled him onto the thicker ice as he backed away from the hole. Later, Ray felt really sorry about losing his good .22 rifle in that deep hole in the swamp. At the time, however, it didn't seem important as he hurried to the cabin. His clothes were beginning to freeze and his teeth were chattering. He was ashamed to face his uncle. He knew he should have listened to his dad and remembered his warnings. He should have been more careful. When he didn't listen to his elders or to his parents he always got into trouble.

Ray's dad, Alec, called him a wanderer because he was independent and would go off by himself. He said, "You go all over the place and you shouldn't do that. It is very dangerous. Sometimes you might meet a bear or something like that."

"I'm not afraid of bears," Ray said.

"You are still a child," he told Ray, "I'm your dad and I'm older than you and you don't understand these things. We have control over this land and the bears too. The bear has no power over us. But you are still a child."

Ray's dad spent many evenings teaching him about the country. Sometimes two or three hours would go by as he taught him. He explained how the creeks all go down to some lake or to some main river, down between the mountains, and he should follow one if he was lost. He warned him about avalanches in the mountains.

"Go along the base of the hill," he cautioned him, "don't ever go along where there are no trees. That is where the avalanche was and it usually comes down in the same place."

Ray listened and learned. He knew his dad was teaching him about safety and how to survive. He warned Ray about thin ice in the fall time when it is starting to freeze and about old rotten ice in the spring time when it starts to thaw. Especially in the spring time, you never know where the soft spots are.

"When you are old enough to sleep alone out in the bush, you are getting old enough to make some decisions for yourself," Ray's dad told him. Ray knew his dad wanted him to prove that he was learning how to take care of himself and be independent on the trapline and in the bush.

"I figure I'm ready to sleep in the bush now," Ray said one day. It was winter when he first stayed out all night by himself. He stayed warm but he didn't sleep much because he heard wolves howling that night. It scared him but he wanted to prove that he could do it and this pleased his dad.

"All right," his dad said, "You have stayed all night in the bush. You know all your traps and the trap lines. Now you are ready to make decisions and take care of yourself." Ray never really felt dependent on his parents after he came back from

Lejac Indian School. He depended on his own decisions and he didn't go back to school.

"I was not afraid in the bush at all," Ray recalled years later. "When I think about how young I was, it was a wonderful experience to wander by myself. I could really think for myself and not depend on anybody."

Ray's dad and grandfather often told him stories about times long ago when the Indian warriors didn't have iron axes and guns. They had rocks and used tomahawks, and spears to kill big game.

"How did you kill the big grizzly bears?" Ray asked.

"Grizzlies never attacked us," his dad said. "Not one Indian was killed by a grizzly. We respect them." Some Indian people believed in witchcraft. Ray's dad did not believe in that. "That is the devil's work," he would say. Ray's dad said that those who believe in witchcraft are not very good and their lives don't end very well. He knew people who believed that way and he got along with them but he believed differently.

The Carrier people had a name for "the one that is up on high." **'Udedoghun** was the Carrier name for the one they respected and wanted to please.

Ray tried to please his parents as he was growing up. He did not want to offend "the one that is up on high" but he did not understand about God's Son who brought salvation. He did not know what the Bible taught about the true "one that is up on high" and His love for all people.

Chapter Eight

Victory in Europe

Ray's older brother Freddie, had followed him into the army, but was not in the same regiment. Between battles, Ray got to see him sometimes, and Freddie told him, "You keep praying and you'll be all right." They had always prayed at home and Ray prayed many times during difficult times in the war.

In Italy they had to drink wine because the water wasn't safe. Sometimes they drank too much, but it wasn't a problem. Ray got along well with the Italian people. In the two years he was there, he learned enough of the language to talk with the people. There was one pretty Italian girl, Fernanda, who was very special to Ray. Ray liked people and when he saw hungry kids in Italy he wanted to help them. When he received a parcel of food or candy, he usually gave it to the kids. Ray really cared about people.

There were some big battles, like Rimini, and an important battle at Monte Casino, where they hit the line and smashed through. Ray's brother, Freddie, was wounded badly in the battle at Monte Casino, in the spring of 1945. They sent him back to Canada. His eardrum was permanently damaged. Ray received wounds twice but he went back to the front lines when he recovered, though he didn't have to. He wanted to see this war won!

That spring in 1945, they went into southern France. Before they went to France, some of them went to a little island, off the coast of Italy called Elba. Ray learned the story of the little warrior, Napoleon, who spent time in exile there, a long time ago.

They hit southern France—the towns of Marseille and Nice and from there on to Lyon. Ray was in a group with American and Canadian soldiers. Some were paratroopers and some were amphibious like Ray's unit. When they got to Nancy, they separated from the rest and joined the First Canadian army in western Europe. The final push was to cross the Rhine River into Germany.

Ray was there when they dropped the paratroopers at Arnhem in the Netherlands. Years later, he saw the Hollywood movie about that battle, called *A Bridge Too Far*. He thought they didn't get it quite right but the movie still brought back bad memories.

There were eight days of intense fighting for control of the Rhine River at Arnhem. The Germans outnumbered the Allied forces and surrounded them. Ray thought the battle would never end. He prayed as he had never prayed before. The Allied forces lost 2500 men and had to retreat after the heavy fighting at Arnhem. Ray helped to ferry wounded and dying men across the river in rubber rafts under the cover of darkness. Each time Ray landed on the river shore for another load of wounded soldiers, he didn't know if the Allied forces or the German army would be there to meet him. There was no time to be scared. He obeyed orders and did what he was ordered to do.

There were more battles in Belgium, the Netherlands, and Germany. Ray went to Utrecht, then into the area of Oldenburg, and finally Hanover that winter. In spring, Allied armies finally closed in on the Germans from all directions and the free world celebrated Victory in Europe, V-E Day, in May, 1945.

Ray was still in Germany after the war was over in Europe. Oldenburg airport was the base for the Canadian army. For several months Ray's job was hauling fuel at this supply base. It troubled him to see all the equipment that the Allied forces destroyed after the war was over. He felt the Canadian and American governments were really wasteful. Mountains of tires, typewriters, binoculars, rifle scopes, and clothing—it was crushed and burned. Ray couldn't understand why they didn't give these things to people who could use them.

Word came that there was room for 200 more Canadians to go on a big ship to Canada. Ray was one of those picked and was soon on his way to Southampton, England. From there he continued the voyage home!

When Ray got back to Canada, the first thing

he did was travel to see his parents in northern British Columbia. It was good to talk to them in the soft Carrier language. His mother prayed for him, rejoicing in his safe return. Other people came to see him and he thanked Wassa Leon for praying for him, too. He respected that great old man.

Ray knew that he could have been killed many different times in the war. At the time he didn't understand that the Lord had kept his life safe for a reason. He was just happy to be home and to see all the family and friends he loved.

While he was in Fort St. James, Ray's dad and uncles planned a spring beaver hunt. Right away the returned soldier wanted to go out trapping with them. While he was overseas, Ray missed being out in the bush and was lonely for the north country and the trap line.

Ray and his family got many beaver on that trip and sold them for a good price. Too soon, the furlough was over and he had to go back to Vancouver. When he was finally discharged from the service in June 1946, Ray was a battle-scarred, experienced warrior. He was almost 23 years old.

Chapter Nine

No longer an Indian

Ray looked at the man from the Indian department with puzzled brown eyes. He frowned as he asked, "What do you mean? Enfranchised? I don't understand."

"You are no longer a member of your Indian band," the official explained. "You were away from the reserve for seven years. You signed away your Indian rights when you joined the Army. So you are on your own now and you can drink booze legally—just like a white man!" He grinned widely to show he thought that would be good news.

Ray stared at the man in disbelief. He was angry and felt like hitting him. How could they say he was not an Indian? Was this the way they treated Indian men who had fought for their country? Tell them they couldn't go home to their own reserve? He believed he'd been fighting this war for freedom! So he could legally drink booze now, he thought bitterly. Well, that's just what he would do.

Ray was only one of many Canadian Indian veterans who came home to a very different world than they had known before World War II. It was estimated that over 6000 Canadian Indians served in that war, despite the fact that they were not citizens. The government policy at the time was to use various means to completely assimilate Native people into the white society.

Ray had six medals from serving in Sicily, Italy, France, Germany, Holland, and Belgium but he had no money. His pay in the Army was nineteen cents a day, unless he got danger pay, which was 25 cents a day!

Ray needed to find a job so he travelled to Vancouver Island and started looking. He got work right away in a logging camp for the MacMillan Bloedel company.

Ray met a girl on Vancouver Island. She was mostly Spanish, but she was also one-eighth Indian. She had grown up in a foster home and her parents liked Ray. She and Ray decided to marry and settled down in Comox on Vancouver Island. Most of the time, Ray was away in logging camps, working for different companies. As the years went by, three little girls were born into the family. They named one little daughter after Ray's girlfriend in Italy. He had told his wife about her and one day she asked, "What was that girl's name in Italy?"

"Fernanda," Ray told her.

"We will call our daughter, Fernanda Marie," she decided. The two other children who followed were named Francis and Florence.

Ray had never before had a problem with drinking too much. It was not legal for Native people to drink in public or buy booze in Canada until several years later (1970). Ray could drink legally now and he began to drink heavily. He drank too much and his wife did too. Life became very hard for them both. Ray said later, "Life became a grind!"

Ray's wife's foster parents, who were concerned, wanted them to go to church. His wife and kids sometimes went with them to the Four Square Gospel church and Ray went along a few times. He didn't feel comfortable there. "Too much exercise!" Ray decided with a twinkle in his eye.

Ray knew he needed a real change in the direction of his life. He had always heard about Jesus but somehow he didn't understand that he needed to know Him in a personal relationship.

"I didn't know how to reach Him," Ray said.

Those years are a difficult memory for Ray. He worked in many different places and it seemed he was always out in the logging camps while his wife and the girls were at home in Comox. The drinking continued and the problems at home didn't get any better. Ray really wanted to make the marriage work for the sake of his children. Though he was making good money, there never seemed to be enough and they were soon behind in paying their bills.

Once, while he lived on Vancouver Island, he went to Victoria and visited with Ed Cozy and his wife Amy, his German neighbours from Fort St. James. They were getting very old and were eager to hear about all the Indian people they had known in the years they lived there. Ray told him about the ones who had died and what he knew about the ones still living. He enjoyed seeing them again and remembering his childhood. No one seemed to bother the Cozys during the war and Ray never really connected them with the terrible war with the Germans in Europe.

Ray decided he would try working on a fishing boat off the coast of British Columbia. He learned the ropes quickly and was beginning to enjoy life on a fishing boat when there was a terrible accident.

While working on the deck, Ray's clothes got tangled in a winch. Before they could stop the motor, his legs and back were caught in the winch and injured terribly. The pain was so bad that Ray was in and out of consciousness.

The crew quickly returned to shore and rushed him to the hospital. As the ambulance raced through the streets with siren blaring, Ray was in such intense pain from his injuries, that he didn't know if he would live or die. Maybe this was the end of his life; it seemed like the worst pain Ray had ever known. He had been near death many times. He wasn't drowned when he went through the ice on the trapline. He had survived the war, survived being wounded twice, made it home. Now this! Would it be the end?

At that time, Ray was not aware that the Bible says that the angels work for God. They are *"sent to help those who are to be saved from the penalty of sin." (Hebrews* 1:14) God had a purpose for this Indian warrior's life. God's angels were watching over Ray.

After surgery, it was weeks before the pain began to lessen. Ray wondered if he would ever walk again; his one twisted knee was especially painful. Ray was glad to be alive. He didn't complain when they sent him to therapy. The months went by as he worked slowly and painfully to regain his strength and to walk again. He was afraid he would never again be able to work. Two full years passed before he could finally leave the hospital rehabilitation centre and go home.

Home was not a pleasant place to be. Things were not any better between him and his wife. He realized his marriage was breaking up and he didn't know what to do. He realized he had been away from his wife and daughters too much. He knew that financially, the situation was very bad. When he got out of the hospital and could look for a job, he thought he owed money to everyone!

Ray got a job at Port MacNeil, on the north end of Vancouver Island, driving a bulldozer at the iron ore mine. He worked hard and kept on working there for 29 months, until he paid off all his bills. It took him more than two long years but he was determined to pay them all and get out of debt.

Ray's dad used to teach him, "When you promise something to somebody, you better come through with it."

"My dad really believed in that. When my dad told someone like the storekeeper that he's going to pay them—he would pay them on that day!" So Ray paid all the debts that he and his wife owed, "even the small ones of ten dollars or so."

Chapter Ten

Searching for the truth

"Come on, Ray. Let's go to the pub. Today has been a hot one!"

"I'll see you later," Ray called to the men on his crew. He walked on down the street and went into the small grocery store. It was an extremely hot day, and they were working hard, clearing the right-of-way for the power line near Terrace, in northern British Columbia.

Ray wasn't sure why he didn't go with the others to drink beer after work that day, as he usually did. He bought some pop and went to sit by the Skeena River to think about things. His dad had always called him a wanderer and he had been wandering around British Columbia for several years. He was getting tired of his way of life.

He had worked in Vancouver in heavy construction after his marriage ended. He was really sorry about the break-up with his wife and he tried to work things out because of his children. He missed his daughters very much. He guessed he had just worked away from home too much. He knew he drank too much and his wife did too.

Ray began wandering around, working at different jobs. He also was searching for the truth and for happiness. He thought that he wanted to know more about Jesus and he knew he needed to change his life. Ray's cousin, Sally, invited him to a Baha'i meeting. When he went back to a second meeting to learn more about it, a woman asked him, "You are single, are you?"

"Yes, I am," Ray answered.

"We are going to get you a wife." She said. "You need to get married and have a wife."

Ray didn't pay much attention to her—he thought she was joking. Soon she brought over a pretty little blonde girl with blue eyes. The girl smiled at Ray and said, "I could be your wife." She seemed to like the looks of this handsome Indian warrior.

"The two of you could go to Iceland to start meetings over there," the other woman said. "We can arrange it pretty quick."

Ray decided this was getting too serious. "I'm not looking for a girl, I can do that for myself, I'm looking for Jesus," Ray said. After he told them this, he got out of there!

Later someone told him, "You cannot leave like that. You cannot just resign from that church."

Ray said, "I never did belong to it in the first place. I just came to see what the meetings were like." That was the end of Ray's relationship with the Baha'i religion. He knew their teachings were not what he was looking for.

Ray didn't want to go to the Roman Catholic Church. He knew he didn't agree with them. He had decided this from experience and from observing their treatment of Indian people through the years. His unhappy memories of residential school were always with him.

"I'm not stupid. When I look at those priests and nuns and what they do—it is not right for me. I don't think you would treat children that way if you are a real Christian. These are educated people I'm talking about and yet they do things that are hard to believe. They overworked children and abused them but they say they believe in God and they figure nothing will happen to them!"

"The turning point in my life was years before, when I saw a priest sin with my own eyes. I was hauling lumber for the priests—helping the Catholic church. They told me if I helped them, I could make it to heaven. When I saw that priest sin, I asked myself: will that same man go up there tomorrow in the church and hold mass with the people? I'm not an educated man, but God showed me that that man was a sinner just like everyone else."

Ray's wandering took him north to Tungsten, in the Northwest Territories. He worked for Canada Tungsten for a summer. From there he went to another mining camp and worked in exploration. He worked there for a year—making roads for the mines, operating a bulldozer. He worked on the construction of the Bennett Dam at Hudson Hope in 1964.

Ray didn't go back home to Fort St. James very often until he learned that his dad had cancer. While working on the Bennett Dam, he started making the long drive a couple of times each month to be with his family. He moved to Terrace to work on the power line in 1965.

In his wandering, Ray did not find the truth he was looking for, nor answers to his questions. He always had friends because he liked people and he could always find drinking buddies. However, there was a longing in his heart that was not satisfied.

Through the years, Ray made a lot of money. But he always spent it on booze and would drink until it was gone. He knew he drank too much. As he sat by the Skeena river that day, he made some decisions. He wanted to make changes in his life. "I'll quit this job," he decided. "I'll try to quit drinking. And, I'll go home to my parents in Fort St. James."

When he moved back to Fort St. James, an attractive, young Native girl soon caught Ray's eye. Nellie worked for a white couple and walked back and forth to work from her home on the reserve. Ray sometimes offered her a ride home. One time he asked her if she would like to go with him to a bingo in Prince George.

"Well, I don't know," Nellie answered, "I'll have to see if it's okay with my mom to go."

Ray understood her hesitation. No matter how old Carrier girls were, they respected their parents. The Native girls were taught to listen and obey their parents, even when they were grown. They accepted that their parents knew what was best for them.

Nellie grew up in a big family of ten kids and though her dad often drank, he always provided for his family.

Nellie was shy and didn't talk much to people. Though she worked for some white people, she was very uncomfortable around them. She learned Ray was a person she could talk to easily. She felt he was an understanding friend. Nellie needed a friend. Ray was older than her and more experienced in the ways of the world. She had experienced some hurts in her nineteen years but with Ray she felt safe.

Ray was working in construction out in the bush, around Takla Lake or wherever the union sent him. Whenever he was in town he spent most of his time with Nellie. She knew he was married before but that didn't seem important to her. She soon looked forward to seeing this handsome warrior with the sparkling brown eyes and big smile. Sometimes they went out drinking even though Ray was trying to quit. They grew to care for each other very much.

Ray's father died in 1967. He was seventy-six years old. Ray was very glad that he had come home to Fort St. James. At the time of family sadness, he was there for his mother and the rest of his family.

Ray met another person after he came home to Fort St. James. Through this encounter, Ray's life changed in a way he never expected!

Chapter Eleven

Choosing life

Ray saw the stranger first in the post office. "That must be the white man who is learning the Carrier language," he thought. Someone said the man needed people to help him translate the Bible. Ray decided that he would like to know more about this. He wasn't shy about getting acquainted.

"I'm Ray Prince," he said, "I hear you want people to help you learn our language."

"Yes, I do," the man replied. "My name is Dick Walker. Why don't you come over to my home and we'll talk about it." They walked to the house where Ray met Dick's wife Shirley. The two men sat down to talk in their living room over coffee.

"I don't know much about the Bible," Ray said, "I know a little about God, and Easter and Christmas. I would like to learn about the Bible. It seems like you know God pretty good."

"Yes, I know God very well." Dick laid the translation materials aside and for the next four hours they talked about God. Ray completely forgot that he was to meet Nellie as he asked Dick some of the questions that had been bothering him for so long. Nellie wondered what was keeping Ray when he didn't come.

Dick gave Ray a New Life Testament to read, written in simple English. Ray took it with him to his heavy equipment job in construction, out in the bush. Often Ray would call Dick with questions.

"What is a prophet?" he asked. "And do you have to wear those 'monkey suits' to attend your church?"

Dick assured him that God didn't care what he wore. "God loves me, just the way I am. God loves you, just the way you are. You don't have to clean up your life to get ready. God wants you to come to Him, just the way you are right now."

Ray felt relieved at that answer. He had been in churches where a suit and tie seemed to be the uniform of the day.

Ray wore out more than one copy of the New Life Testament as he read and wondered. The questions became more personal as Ray read his Bible and the Holy Spirit spoke to his heart. Ray knew he was a sinner; he knew he had sinned.

"Will God forgive me, even if I have killed people?" Ray knew he had killed many people during the war. He had packed his medals away because they reminded him of that terrible war.

"Paul killed Christians," Dick replied, "but the Lord saved him." Ray thought he remembered reading something about that.

Another thing really troubled him and he asked Dick, "What about separation and divorce?" Ray told Dick about his first marriage.

Dick explained that God hates divorce (Malachi 2:16) but we can ask God to forgive us. "When you receive the Lord Jesus Christ into your life," Dick said. "Your new life starts right there. God promises you that He will forgive you if you confess your sins to him. You start with a clean page in God's book." This gave Ray a lot to think about.

The game warden came to Ray with a suggestion. "Your brother, Teddy, is going to lose his guiding license. He has been drinking heavily and can't keep up with his guiding business. Why don't you take it over?"

"I'm not a big game guide," Ray told him. "I can hunt but I never guided anyone. I've been working in construction for years since I came back from the war."

The game warden encouraged Ray and said he would give him help getting started. "Okay, I'll give it a try," Ray answered. He began a new life as a big game guide and outfitter.

Ray spent much time out in the bush alone, in his guiding area. As he kept reading his Bible the Lord gradually helped him to understand how much God loved him. One day Ray read in his Bible, *"I am the Way and the Truth and the Life. No one can go to the Father except by Me,"* (John 14:6).

With tears filling his eyes, Ray read another verse. It said, *"For God so loved the world that He gave His only Son. Whoever puts his trust in God's Son will not be lost, but will have life that lasts forever,"* (John 3:16). He began to understand the salvation that was there for him in Jesus Christ.

Ray was getting ready for a fall hunt and there

alone in the cabin, he humbly asked the Lord Jesus for forgiveness and invited Him to come into his life. Ray realized he couldn't straighten out his whole life first. He could only come to Jesus the way he was. The Lord loved him and would help him with the booze and the problems of his past life.

Ray was forty-five years old when he became a Christian. "I accepted the Lord and gave my life to Him that day," he said. "Right there, I decided, I'm going to give Jesus Christ 100 per cent of my life. Not 25 per cent or 60 per cent or 80 per cent, but I will give Him all of my life."

Ray and Nellie had been living with Ray's mom in Fort St. James. A little daughter, Cynthia was born to them. Ray's mother became ill and in 1971 she died. Ray loved his parents and he thought about how they had prepared him by teaching him about God.

"We depend too much on our parents for our religion," he said, many years later. "As long as they are religious and they are praying, we think we are okay. But it is not so. I know now for myself—it is 'one-on-one' with God. Me and God. God in Jesus Christ. He is the one who died for me. I can do a lot of things. I can give money away to the churches, to the poor, and a lot of wonderful deeds, but that won't take me to heaven. Jesus Christ is the only one. He said so in John 14:6. *'I am the Way.'* He said it plainly! That's the verse that brought me to the Lord."

Dick invited Ray along when the missionary and his family went to the United States to a conference at their home church in California. Ray enjoyed this warm, caring group of believers. He decided he wanted to be baptized so he asked the pastor about it. The pastor talked with him and agreed that he should go ahead. Ray was thinking about a simple, quiet service but he was surprised when the congregation was over 750 people. He was a bit nervous as, before he was baptized, he gave his testimony of how the Lord had saved him.

Ray and Nellie began going to the small fellowship group that met in Dick and Shirley's home for Bible study. Ray was a new Christian and he was just starting to learn about the Lord. He had his own business, guiding hunters in the fall and guiding fishermen in the summers. They lived in Fort St. James but Ray still spent time working out in the bush.

"A person like me has to spend his own time alone, when he's thinking about decisions like that. He has to go out by himself and retreat. I did that right after I was saved. I used to go out alone to my guiding area."

"God speaks to us, you know. I was reading my Bible and He was right there telling me what He means by the things He says there in His Word. Through the Holy Spirit, He is teaching us. I spent week after week up there and the Lord really taught me."

Chapter Twelve

Growing in Christ

Nellie helped Ray build up his guiding business in the Nation Lakes area. They built two cabins at Tchentlo Lake. They had plywood and lumber flown in. It was expensive to build those cabins. Later they built cabins at Chuchi Lake and Inzana Lake. Nellie loved spending time out in the bush. Two more little ones were born into the family. Cynthia, Rachel, and Joseph spent each summer and fall with their parents at the hunting camp.

Ray advertised his outfitting business in the hunting magazines. Most of the hunters who came were American and Germans. "Those West German guys are the ones who really got me established in my guiding area. They sure liked western Canada and they are really good hunters, too. They have good ideas about hunting." Ray put aside all the bad memories of the war with Germans and accepted each of the hunters as individuals.

Dick asked Ray to go with him for a few days to a translation workshop in Medicine Hat, Alberta. Ray had never seen so many people, Native and white, from so many different backgrounds. They were all there to learn about translation but they were not all Christians. Ray was an eager new Christian and he just couldn't understand some of their beliefs. Dick tried to explain the difference to him.

"Some of them are like the Jews. They saw that Jesus was one of them, they saw Him work miracles. They saw God work miracles—God parted the Red Sea for them to escape—but they still don't believe in Jesus."

He met some Christians there—Navajos, Apaches, and Indians from Mexico. "We even sang with the Navajos," Ray said, "And we recognized the similarities of our languages."

While Ray was growing in his Christian life, Nellie had not yet made a decision to become a Christian. He didn't pressure her about it. When he travelled to gatherings of Christians, she sometimes came along. Other times she stayed at home with the children. She was still very uncomfortable around white people or crowds of people.

There were some new missionaries in the area, besides the Wycliffe translators, Dick and Shirley Walker. Some of them wanted help in learning Carrier. Nellie and Ray had been helping with the language work. Dave Wilkinson and Dick Walker were working on a Carrier dictionary. Nellie transcribed some taped stories they got from the Native people. She worked on the Carrier literacy program and helped with an oral manual to use in the schools. Sometimes, she didn't know a word but Ray would work with her.

It was difficult for Nellie to feel at ease with the white missionaries. Ray would say to her in Carrier, "Talk to them" but she found it hard to do that. Gradually, she realized that they accepted her and Ray just the way they were. It made no difference whether they were white or Native. The missionaries liked them as persons and friends. Gradually, she understood the love of God as these new friends showed her they cared.

One day Dick asked Nellie if she had ever given her life to the Lord. Nellie said, "No." She had always thought, "How could I be a Christian when I am not even accepted in the Catholic church? Ray was married before and we are living together."

Dick and Shirley told her, "The Lord will take you just as you are. He doesn't just change you overnight to be the way He wants you to be. After you accept Him, you will grow, just like a baby. It takes time for a baby to grow and learn, and that is what we are like."

The Lord had prepared Nellie's heart and she knew she needed to receive Him into her life. She made a decision to give her life to Jesus Christ.

Dick had not been aware that Ray and Nellie were living together as an unmarried couple. When he learned about this, Dick showed Ray these verses in his Bible.

"If we tell Him our sins, He is faithful and we can depend on Him to forgive us our sins. He will make our lives clean from all sin. If we say we have

not sinned, we make God a liar and His Word is not in our hearts," (1 John 1:9-10).

"Don't call God a liar and say you have no sin," Dick said, gently.

"I was waiting for you to talk to me about it." Ray replied, quietly. The Holy Spirit had been speaking to Ray and Nellie and they knew they needed to straighten out their lives. So they made things right and soon they married. The wedding was there in Dick's home.

Ray and Nellie continued to grow in their love for the Lord and for each other. Though there was more than 20 years difference in their ages it never seemed a problem. They enjoyed their young family and took them everywhere with them. Nellie wanted to raise her own children and teach them about the Lord. She did not want to depend on her parents to raise them, as the custom was of some traditional Native families.

Nellie and Ray worked well together—in Bible translation, budgeting their money, teaching their kids, and travelling together.

"Just like the beaver," Ray said, remembering his trapping days. "When you take the female, the male beaver looks all over for her. When we both belong to the Lord we are a team. We do everything together."

"I thought a lot about our marriage," Ray said. "I didn't want to have a second mistake. I realized Nellie was lots younger than me but we worked it out pretty good and are raising the children for the Lord. We are both Christians and that made the difference. I was not a Christian when I was married before and I did not teach my children, my daughters, about the Lord but I am praying for them."

Ray's first wife had died but he kept in touch with his grown daughters. Florence, lived in northern B.C. for a few months but it was unfamiliar to her and she moved back to Vancouver Island. Another daughter lived in the Queen Charlotte Islands and the third lived in Toronto so Ray did not see them often.

One highlight each fall for Ray, was a trip to Quesnel, B.C. to the Native Family Bible Conference. For several years, this conference was at the Native Bible Centre, a small Christian school in central B.C. Native Christians came from all over British Columbia. They crowded into the log buildings for a weekend, to encourage one another and to share the needs of their hearts. The speaker was always a Native Christian—sometimes Bill Jackson or Vincent Yellow Old Woman from Alberta, Joe Jolly or Stan Williams from Ontario. Josh Harjo and Frank Duncan, Indian preachers from the U.S. came too.

A Native preacher who spoke there once said, "It is a sin to worry." Ray was still a new Christian and that helped him to grow in his walk with the Lord. "That said something to me," Ray remembers. "I thought about things a lot—problems in my life—and how to solve them as a human being will. So I never worry anymore."

The speaker also said it was a sin to gamble. Nellie loved to play bingo and went regularly. After she heard that, she quit going to bingo. "That's gambling," she decided.

ets, too. "No tickets," Ray said, "because we trust the Lord. Once you start buying those tickets, you aren't trusting the Lord."

Along with other native believers, Ray and Nellie found these times of fellowship refreshing and helpful. "The native conferences we have are uplifting," Ray maintained. "You rejoice with one another and when you came back home here you are all charged up again."

Ray longed to go to Bible school, but felt he didn't have enough education. He learned from the missionaries and other Christians.

"The missionaries helped us a lot," he said. "This is how I learned. Those people teach me. They teach me from the Bible and I search it out for myself. I iron all that out and today I am standing firm with the Lord."

"Before I was saved, I thought all Christians were crazy. Once they were building a road to Tachie and it was a terrible, muddy road. A guy was towing a small mobile home, a trailer, trying to go up that road and his trailer was really stuck in the mud. I had my mother with me and I thought 'What a stupid guy!' I didn't know that guy was Fred Brown, the new missionary that was moving to Tachie. He helped me study the Bible a lot after I became a Christian.'

"These missionaries have love in their hearts for the people. They don't try to destroy us, they want to save us. That was different from the Catholic priests and nuns and that encouraged me."

"I thought about these people who had come here to be missionaries to the Indian people. They have education and are intelligent and could have many degrees, and maybe make a lot of money. Why are they here? There must be something more important to them. It must be Jesus Christ!"

Chapter Thirteen

No fighting back

"You are going straight to hell and you won't even stop in purgatory!" Ray's neighbour had been drinking and the booze loosened his tongue. He knew Ray was a Christian and no longer went to the Catholic church. The neighbour didn't like that.

Ray almost punched the guy in the face. He stood by his truck and tried to calm down. He wanted to fight back but he knew God would not approve of that! God was his Commander now and he would obey God's Word.

The more Ray learned from God's Word, the more he knew with certainty that God had protected him throughout his whole life. Psalm 139 said "even in his mother's womb" God knew all his days. He realized he could have drowned when he fell through the ice, or died in the war, or died when he was on the fishing boat. God must have a purpose for his life and Ray would trust Him to keep on taking care of his problems.

Since Ray and Nellie had become Christians, some of their family and many people on the reserve had turned against them. Everyone knew that they were Christians. Everyone watched their daily lives. Some gave them the "silent treatment". Others were more outspoken. Many native people tried to scare them into returning to the Roman Catholic Church. It was difficult, both for Ray and Nellie and for their children. Ray became a bit fearful. People kept reminding him of his past life.

"It was terrible! They ridiculed me and accused me but I knew the Lord had changed me. They kept reminding me of my old, sinful life. I wanted my life to be different. Sometimes it was a tough struggle but I am bravest when Christ is with me, and I am the worst coward without Him."

It was hard for Ray to keep from fighting back. The Lord was in command of his life and Ray looked to Him daily to guide him and give him strength. The missionaries taught them from God's Word when they were home. But they spent time in summer fishing season and fall hunting season at the hunting camp, away from Fort St. James. When the children started school, the other kids teased and bullied them. The family tried to go to the hunting camp often where it was peaceful.

The logging companies were moving into the area. This began to make a big change in Ray's guiding business. The noise and activity in the woods were making the animals leave for other places. Things were changing quickly.

Ray and Nellie needed to find another place to live. There was no running water or bathroom in their house. Nellie was expecting their fourth child and it was hard packing water when Ray was away guiding. It seemed they could find no other place to live in Fort St. James. Winter was coming on, so they talked about what they should do. They decided to move to Prince George, a growing city about 100 miles to the south.

"It just seemed like the Lord was telling us to get out of there," Ray said. "We were not strong Christians and it was hard. There were no missionaries in Prince George at all then and some people thought we were making a big mistake. We didn't have any of the missionaries to teach us after we moved, but we learned to trust the Lord more."

Ray still had his guiding business and they still went out to the cabin in the summer to guide fishermen. After they moved, they visited different churches in Prince George but they were not too comfortable with people who seemed to feel it important to be "dressed up." Many weekends they went back out in the bush to the hunting camp.

The second year they lived in Prince George, some new missionaries moved there with the plan to establish a native church. Ray and Nellie worked alongside Bill and Maggie Farmer and Alan and Linda Ross to win people to the Lord and get the native church started. Ray and Nellie encouraged the missionaries and enjoyed Christian fellowship with these Christians. Ray and Nellie were still hurting from the way they had been treated in Fort St. James. As more native people came to the Lord, they grew stronger. It felt good to be part of God's family in the Prince George native church and with the missionaries.

Every morning Ray read his Bible "to get encouragement and direction from his Commander" for the day. He prayed for knowledge to share with others about Jesus Christ. He saw all the native people who lived in Prince George, or who came there for jobs or schooling. He thought about his relatives and friends that lived at Fort St. James and on the reserves.

"Our native people don't have just money problems or other kinds of problems. The real problem is that they do not know the Lord's way. I try to share with them the way of salvation in Jesus Christ. I pray for tools I need to serve Him, any way I can."

Ray often met native people on the street in Prince George. He wanted to share about Jesus with the ones who needed Him.

"I met a Carrier friend in town one day. Usually he was drunk but this time he was sober. 'I am glad you are sober today'" Ray said, "'I used to drink, too, but I don't drink anymore. Let's go have coffee and talk about it.'"

As Ray told this man about the Lord, the man said he knew about Him.

"Why don't you go the Lord's way? Start over and be a Christian, like me?" Ray asked him.

"My parents would not want me to do that," he said.

"But you are 50 years old," Ray said, "and you have to decide for yourself. What does the cow moose do when the moose gets to be two years old? She pushes him out! You have to make up your own mind." Ray knew it was a hard decision for native people. Often their family would not approve. He trusted the Holy Spirit to work in hearts.

Eventually, Ray decided he had to sell his guiding business. Business was not good. The logging companies had built roads and moved in their heavy equipment and trucks and the animals were moving out. It spoiled the hunting and he felt that they forced him out of business. Taxes had increased and he was glad when he found a buyer. He sold the six cabins and the outfitting business for enough to pay all his bills. It was hard to let go of the hunting camp. Ray and Nellie and their family had many pleasant memories of the time they spent there.

Ray had good memories of the winters spent in that area with his parents on the trap line. For three or four months each winter, they were in a world of their own at Inzana Lake. In the native language "inzanun" means the time in March when the sun comes up in the morning at the east end of the lake and the shadow goes straight to the other end. In the evening it is just the opposite.

The trapline had belonged to his family for generations. Ray inherited the trapline from his father and grandfather but those days on the trapline were gone and things were changing rapidly. As Ray learned from the Bible, he began to realize that his most important inheritance comes from his heavenly Father.

Life in Prince George was a big change for Ray. He had worked hard all his life. He had operated a bulldozer, ten hours a day on some jobs, and for 31 years he belonged to The International Union of Operating Engineers. Hunting and guiding kept him active in the bush—from daylight until dark. He missed the green and golden fall time and leading the hunters to where the moose fed along the lakes.

City life was different. Ray had trouble feeling at home in a big apartment building bordered by dirty sidewalks and noisy city streets. He longed for the crisp mountain air instead of the sour smell from the pulp mills there in Prince George.

They often had some of their family visit from the reserve. Nellie's youngest brother, Owen, spent most of his time with them. He travelled with them and went to the native family camps. They rejoiced when he received the Lord into his life.

Ray enjoyed his young family. The boys liked to play hockey and he was always there for their practices or when they had a game. Silas and Rebecca had been born into the family and with the activities of five lively children, Ray kept busy and didn't get bored. Still, Ray wasn't keeping physically active. His usual activities were Bible studies, travelling and witnessing for the Lord, and teaching his children.

"I was changing as I read the Bible every day to find my answers to life," Ray said. "I would read the Bible until my eyes were sore. I became a different person by reading the Word of God."

"After I accepted the Lord, a new life began for me. I realized how many mistakes I had made in my past life. I try to correct that every day and help people. I love people and I have no hatred for anybody. I forgive people that have done me wrong."

Ray didn't realize that his love for people and his ability to forgive would soon be put to the test.

Chapter Fourteen

The power of forgiveness

Ray was in the Prince George hospital again, in intensive care. This was his second heart attack and Ray was groggy and confused from the strong medicine they gave him. He thought he saw the face of someone he knew.

"That couldn't be the same guy," Ray thought, "I must be dreaming. That guy, Don, is not around here."

Back at home a couple of weeks later, he was feeling better when he saw the hospital chaplain, a local pastor.

"They brought a man from the correctional centre to the hospital here in Prince George," the chaplain said. "He is very sick, paralysed, can't talk, and may not live much longer. I am sure he is the man who stole your truck."

When he heard that, Ray knew that he had seen

Don in the hospital. He prayed, "Lord, what should I do?"

He remembered when Don had first come to Prince George. He knew Ray's nephew, Ken, and called him his "brother." Ken and his wife were new believers and they brought Don with them to the native fellowship. The Indian Christians made this white guy welcome and he came back to the services and listened. Ray talked to him about the Lord and he seemed interested.

One day, Don announced, "I have been promised a job on the Alaska highway as a supervisor. I don't know what to do; I have no way to get to the Yukon and no money. If I can go and take the job, I will get Ken a job there, too."

Native people are always ready to share with someone who needs help. They didn't have much themselves but the Christians gave him warm clothing, boots, and loaned him $200 travel money. Ray loaned his 4x4 pickup and Don loaded it with extra tires, chain saw, Ken's tools and his belongings.

The people of the fellowship liked Don and were glad that he had a job. They had prayer with him one Sunday and he left Monday morning with the promise that he would return the pickup the next weekend. The weekend came but no Don and no pickup! The second week passed and still nothing—no message. This troubled Ray. Ken said he was afraid there had been an accident or some trouble on the road. They all prayed for Don's safety.

Finally, Ray called the Yukon highway department. They said, "No—there is no Don B—working here. We never promised him a job."

Ray was really angry. He felt like Don had used him—ripped him off! Ray knew in the old days, before he was a Christian, he would have planned to get even—to get revenge. He knew that wouldn't be right but he didn't know what to do, so he prayed. He called the insurance company and asked them what he should do. They told him he should report it to the RCMP as a stolen vehicle if Don didn't return. Ray waited a few more days, then he reported it.

One day as Ray was reading his Bible, the Lord directed his attention to these verses:

"But I gave up those things that were so important to me for Christ. Even more than that, I think of everything as worth nothing. It is so much better to know Christ Jesus my Lord. I have lost everything for Him. And I think of these things as worth nothing so that I can have Christ. I want to be as one with Him.... I was made right with God by faith in Christ," (Philippians 3:7-9).

"I began to understand that things like my pickup were just like nothing compared to knowing my Lord," Ray said. "I kept praying and the Lord began to give me peace. I felt sure He would work it out for good just like He says in verse 28 of Romans 8. *"We know that God makes all things work together for the good of those who love Him and are chosen to be a part of His plan."*

"Even my wife Nellie had trouble believing that I wasn't angry," Ray recalls. The other Native believers watched him, too. They kept praying for Don as weeks went by.

In time, the RCMP found the winch and

canopy off Ray's pickup in the Yukon. After a couple of months, they found the pickup near Pelly Crossing, in Yukon Territory. It showed 18,000 extra kilometres on the odometer dial and the truck was in pretty bad shape. Ray made a cold bus trip north in February to drive his pickup back home.

The RCMP charged Don with the theft, but he didn't show up for the court case. Ray had not heard anything more about him, but the RCMP had arrested him, and now he was in the hospital!

When Ray got to the hospital, he hesitated. The nurse said Don was on life-support and was drifting in and out of consciousness. There was a limit on visitors and she said he couldn't stay long. Later they told Ray, they didn't expect Don to live more than 24 hours.

The man was Don! He looked like skin and bones, with tubes and bottles that seemed to tie him to the bed. When he saw Ray, his eyes grew wide with surprise and he seemed afraid.

Ray began to talk to him, "We love you and God loves you. The native fellowship has been praying for you."

Then Ray said, "I forgive you for taking my truck. Because God forgave me, I forgive you, and I'm not angry, I have been praying for you." Tears came from Don's eyes and Ray knew he understood what he was saying. He couldn't talk or move. The nurse came to say that it was time to leave.

Ray went back the next day and brought his Bible and read to Don. He told him again that God loved him, that the native people were praying, and that he forgave him. Nellie came along too. She couldn't believe that Ray was being so patient with Don. She knew that the Lord had changed Ray!

Don still couldn't talk and was sometimes asleep or unconscious when they went to see him. Ray kept going each day. He prayed that the Lord would give Don enough time to understand God's love and to receive Christ into his heart.

One day, the nurse said that they had notified Don's family back east and the doctor was going to remove the life support system. It was just a matter of time until he would be gone. That night all the Christians prayed again for Don. The next day all the tubes had been removed—but he didn't seem worse. The next day he seemed stronger and each day there he seemed to improve. He began to recover his speech and slowly feeling came back to his body.

After almost five weeks, Don could talk enough to tell Ray he believed in Christ as his Saviour and wanted to live as a Christian! Everyone was happy because they knew the Lord answered prayer. Don looked forward to their visits and hearing the Bible read. Ray could see that forgiveness has strong power.

One Sunday morning, the native church service was just beginning. They were singing praises to God when a taxi stopped in front of the building. The driver got out and helped someone to get into a wheelchair. Don was still very weak and pale but he managed to come into the service that morning and speak to the people.

"I'm sorry," he said, with tears, "Please forgive me." Don later went back east to his family but Ray received a letter from him at Christmas. He was still doing well.

"I could forgive Don because God, in Christ Jesus, has forgiven me," Ray said. Don is now a child of God and he is forgiven. Like it says in Ephesians 4:32: *"You must be kind to each other. Think of the other person. Forgive other people just as God forgave you because of Christ's death on the cross...."*

Ray's sister, Lisette Pierre, lived at Fort St. James. She heard about Ray's stolen pickup and his forgiveness of Don. She told the story to some native people in a prayer meeting.

"Why do we have so many grudges?" She asked them. "The Lord will not listen to us if we hate our brothers and our sisters. My brother loved that man that stole his truck and that man came to know the Lord. That's what we should be doing!"

Chapter Fifteen

A different battle

What did you do to Philip? "Ray's cousin, Josephine, asked. It was Christmas and she had called from Fort St. James. Ray wondered what was wrong. He knew she didn't drink but her husband, Philip, drank a lot and he was often in trouble.

"I haven't done anything to him, that I know of," Ray answered. He sounded worried.

"Ray," she said, "I have been married to this man many years. This is the first time in my life that he is sitting here sober, having Christmas dinner with me and he looks good."

"Josie," Ray said, "I didn't do anything to Philip. I just told him about Jesus. I told him, 'Jesus is the only one who can change your life.'"

Philip had a real drinking problem for years. He would sometimes be attacked, beaten, and robbed when he was drinking. Every fall he would be out on his snowmobile and would have an accident—or tip it over and get hurt. Once, he broke his arm and had to have a pin in it—he usually broke some bone. He seemed impossible. The doctor in Vanderhoof would say "You again? When are you going to learn?"

Once he was on the trapline with Ray near Airline Lake. He was breaking trail and Ray prayed, "Jesus, please change that man's life." Now Philip had become a Christian. He and his family started going to the Carrier Fellowship near Tachie.

"I know he has fallen two or three times since he became a Christian," Ray said. "I told him we loved him and were glad when he came back to the Lord. But I said, 'I prayed for you and I never gave up on you. How do you think God feels when you hurt him like that? You told me you accepted the Lord and He said He will never leave you. I am tired of you getting drunk and then saying you are sorry. Maybe God is tired of you, too.' After that, Philip got straightened out and he is living for the Lord today. Drinking is not a problem any more."

Though memories of World War II linger in Ray's mind, his battles are different now. He travelled around the western provinces with a young man who was making a documentary film about the native war veterans. "They are forgotten soldiers," Ray says. Many live in poverty, terrible conditions, and the government is not helping them. Some don't know how to get help. Ray wants to help change that situation. He feels the native veterans were never recognized properly for the part they played in the war.

Ray was invited to go to Europe for an anniversary with some of the Native veterans. He walked with his daughter among the crosses on the battlefield at Normandy. "You know, there are 75,000 Canadians buried at Normandy. There were heavy casualties and the average age was 22 years old on those crosses. Some 19 or 20 but 35 was really old. I thought how sad it was. It was the same with all the veterans that were there. One guy said, 'These guys are the people that really paid the price. We were just fortunate; we are just lucky to be alive." Ray knows that the Lord kept him alive for a reason.

Though the battles and the battlefields are changed, but Ray is still a warrior. His dark hair in sprinkled with grey and his limp causes him to walk more slowly. He has some problem with his lungs because he had pneumonia several times and he has been in the hospital often. He must constantly have extra oxygen from a portable unit. He has survived two heart attacks.

"When I was overseas I was not a Christian. Yet, the Lord had His hand on me all the time. I could have been killed many times. Since then I read in the Bible that God chose me, even in my mother's womb. He chose me to be a Christian and he meant for me to be a leader for the Native people here in Prince George. A Native Christian leader! He is my Commander and I obey Him!"

"We must make ourselves available to God. He must come first in our lives; we always make Him number one. Whatever we do—before our families, before our loved ones, before our friends—

we put God first. Then we can start working with our native people, telling them about the Lord."

"I talk to young people. I believe in the young people; they are our future. I would be selfish if I didn't pray for them and love them. I want to lead them to know the Lord at an early age. Then we will have good leaders in the future for the church and for the Lord's work. Who is going to teach them? There is no one but us. Parents must teach their children."

"We were at the native family camp at Houston, BC. Many native elders came to camp and they seemed hungry for the Word of God. I never before heard them asking questions like they asked. It is because of the breakdown of trust in the Catholic leaders."

"Some priests were brought to court for abusing kids in the residential schools. The native elders say, 'Who can we trust? We trusted the priests and look what happened. The Roman Catholic Church let us down. Who can we trust now?'

"I told them, 'You can only trust Jesus Christ.'

"I don't understand why these priests get a high-priced lawyer. If they are Christians, why don't they just kneel down—in front of the congregation—and say, 'Father, I have sinned against you. Forgive me my sin.' That's what the Bible says we should do. When I was a child and went to the residential school, all these things were happening. They did many things that were wrong but the church would cover it over or pretend that nothing happened. Now these things are revealed and they are wide open. People need to know the truth.

"The Bible says, *'If I cherish sin in my heart, the Lord will not listen'* (Psalm 66:18). We must confess our sin and ask the Lord to forgive.

"There is no hope in the Roman Catholic teaching. It is like looking at a wall. There is no way to get through; there is no help. They say if your marriage breaks up you are condemned to hell. That's the end to this road; you are going to hell. They don't tell us there is hope in Jesus Christ. The Catholic church thinks they brought God to us but they only brought their religion. My people knew about God for a long time before that. Now they need to know Jesus."

Chapter Sixteen

No fear of the future

"I just come from visiting a guy in the hospital," Ray said one day. "He has been there two or three years, I think. I go to visit him often. He was drinking and in a bad accident and injured his spine. It is sad. He lays there on his back and can only turn on the television with his mouth."

"Alfred," I said, "I come here to pray for you."

"So he quickly turned off the television and I prayed for him. I prayed that the Lord would comfort him. Then I talked to him about the Lord."

"There is nobody else that can help you. No one else can save you but the Lord. Other people might tell you that something else can help you, but only Jesus Christ can help you. You better trust Him. That booze is why you are here."

Ray often goes to the hospital to visit with native people. He is concerned about so many people being on drugs and alcohol. His brother, Teddy, died of the effects of his alcoholism. Ray doesn't know how, but he wishes there was a way to stop the alcohol and drugs. He knows it is like a bad disease and he prays for the native people, especially the young people. He knows they need the Lord in their lives to give them strength.

"In 1987, my MLA (provincial legislator) finally got me reinstated as a member of my former band. Now, I have Indian status but the band treats me like an outsider. They said the policy had changed and since we are not living on the reserve, they could not help with my daughter's college expenses. I think it is because she is going to the Christian college—a Bible college." Paying the price for being a Christian is still part of Ray's world.

Living in Prince George was so different from the reserve; he doesn't always know what is going on in the city. On the reserve, everyone knew what happened last night. When someone was in trouble, everyone knew about it right away. Ray missed that, but they have many friends in the city and their home became a gathering place for native friends.

Ray was careful to teach his kids. "My children are growing up in the city but I still warn them of dangers. They still need to learn to listen to their elders. I tell them, 'Look, your friends might give you a sip of booze, even a little one, and tell you it won't hurt. That's the one that hurts! Don't try it, it's no good. Don't try drugs! If you try just a little bit and you want more—you are hooked!'

My kids tell me, 'Daddy, when I don't listen to you, I get in trouble or I have an accident!'

"One time we were up at my guiding area and we had the snowmobile there on the ice. The lake was frozen. Joe was small and he wanted to drive the snowmobile. I decided to let him. I told him, 'you will be okay as long as you stay on the lake and keep on the trail where the skidoo has been before.' 'Okay,' he said. So he went around once and then he decided to come inland. The first thing, he ran into a building. He almost busted his head open, had a big cut and smashed one ski of the skidoo. I think he learned his lesson. Another time he cut a tendon, using a knife. He learned some hard lessons.

"You have to teach kids to listen. I tried not to get mad but they must be told and they must learn to listen. Especially listen to God. Open your Bible every day. My oldest boy, Joe, was counseling in the Christian camp. He really cares about the kids and always smiles and has patience. He has been listening.

"My brother, Norman, is helping Dick translate the Bible into our language. Once he told me, 'Ray, I'm pretty sick and got to have an operation. If I don't make it will you take care of my family?' I prayed for Norman and then I told him, 'I will do that, but don't worry. I think you are going to make it and God is going to use you. You are reading the Gospel and helping to translate it. You will learn to trust Him.' Today, he is healthy and he is older than I am.

"One thing my mother and dad taught me is 'Never believe in defeat—never practice it'. That's what the Bible teaches too. Never give up. Don't give in to Satan. God gives us power and we are more than conquerors (Romans 8:37). He gives us the victory in Jesus Christ to have power over sin," (1 Corinthians 15:57).

Ray and Nellie have travelled many miles to minister for Christ. Ray goes to many different places to share with Native people how the Lord has changed his life. Wherever he is invited—Quesnel, Hazelton, or Prince Rupert, he will go. "I go and I'm always patient because if it's God's will, He will put gas in my tank. I don't ask for any money. I trust Him and He takes care of me."

Ray can say with Paul, *"We thank God for the power Christ has given us. He leads us and makes us win in everything. He speaks through us wherever we go . . ."* (2 Corinthians 2:14).

"I am on the front line in this battle. The missionaries and other Christians support me by encouraging me, and praying for me. I need that supply line. They led me to the Lord and explained God's Word to me. Every day I ask God not to let me get into sin. If I get into sin it would hurt the Christian people who are praying for me. But more than that it would make the Holy Spirit sad."

Ray has learned the truth found in Ephesians 6 about the armour of God and the things God gives his warriors to fight with. He knows that Christians can fight against the spirits of darkness in this world if they are protected. They must be right with God, have the shield of faith to put out the flaming arrows of the devil, and use the sword of the Spirit, which is the Word of God.

"I just read Psalm 37 this morning," Ray said. "I figure those who oppose us are weightless, you know. With God they are nothing—just like smoke. I just trust the Lord."

"I talk with God every day. I pray every morning that everything will work out according to His plan. That is how I pray. I ask for forgiveness of sin. That is how I live every day. I pray for my children and family, and for other Christians. I pray for our leaders—political leaders at all levels. I pray especially for Native leaders that will come to know the Lord and put Him first. They need to make Him number one and ask God what He wants them to do."

"There are a lot of things I would like to do with the rest of my life," Ray tells us. "When I had my heart attack, I talked with the Lord. 'If you want to take me now, you can. It's up to your will and you know better than I do. There are some things I would like to do yet. I want to finish raising my children for you. I would like to get a church building for the Native church to be established here in Prince George. We have some money in the bank—a building fund. We need to have our own place to meet so the Native people know where to go.

"I would like to bring more of our Native people to the Lord, especially the young people. I want to help them learn the Word of God so that they can help themselves to have a new life. That's what I want to do.'"

Ray fights the powers of darkness and recognizes the Enemy. He knows that Satan wants to hinder him from leading Native people to the Lord. He fights spiritual battles, praying for his brothers and sisters in the Lord's family. He prays for the missionaries who are faithfully sharing the good news of salvation with the Native people and teaching them God's word.

Ray's life illustrates how a person passes from darkness into light. When he became a Christian, his life completely changed and he began to follow Christ. Ray has the gift of encouragement. He encourages his family and friends, his brothers and sisters in Christ. He tells them, "Nellie and I are praying for you." He rejoices when he hears about answers to prayer. Once he was travelling on the train and he met a Christian native man from Lillooet in southern British Columbia.

"How are things going there?" Ray asked. When he heard that people had been turning to the Lord and studying God's Word, he rejoiced that his prayers were answered. He had been praying for the missionaries and native people there for many years.

"The main thing about Ray's life is his consistent testimony and witness for Christ," Dick Walker says. "Many native people have professed to receive Christ and then fallen. I can point to Ray and Nellie as an example of those who have consistently followed the Lord and taught others about Him."

Recently, Ray stood before the native church in Prince George to speak. "Stand firmly for the Lord," he encouraged the people. "Be steadfast, don't retreat. This has been a discouraging time for me. I am waiting for some test results about my health problems. I didn't die in the battles I have been through, because God wanted to use me. He is in control of my future. Whether the report is good or bad, it doesn't matter. I belong to Jesus Christ and I have no fear of the future."

EMMAUS CORRESPONDENCE SCHOOL

If you would like to begin studying the Bible, Emmaus Correspondence School is offering a twelve lesson correspondence course entitled BORN TO WIN to those who are currently in prison. This course is specifically designed for prisoners.

Write to: Born to Win, Indian Life Ministries
PO Box 3765 RPO Redwood Centre
Winnipeg, MB R2W 3R6 Canada

My name is _____

Address _____

Town _____

Prov/State _____ Postal/Zip _____

FREE BIBLE OFFER

For Those in Prison

Indian Life Ministries would like to send you a free Bible if you are currently in prison and are interested in what God's Word has to say to you. To receive your free Bible, write to:

Write to: Indian Life Ministries
PO Box 3765 RPO Redwood Centre
Winnipeg, MB R2W 3R6

My name is _____

Address _____

Town _____

Prov/State _____ Postal/Zip _____

A PRAYER OF INVITATION

If you feel that God is speaking to you and you would like to accept Jesus Christ as your personal Savior, please pray the following prayer. You can also say this prayer in your own words.

"Dear Jesus, I realize I am a sinner. I long for peace in my heart. I believe you are the Holy Son of God, that you came down and died on the cross for my sins. Thank you for doing this for me. I am sorry for my sins. Please forgive me. With your help, I will turn my back on them. By faith, I receive you into my life as my personal Saviour and Lord. From now on, I want to please you."

If you have followed these steps and asked Christ to take control of your life, get a copy of God's Word, the Bible, and begin reading it. Also start talking to God in prayer. Go to church regularly. Choose a church where God's message of salvation is taught.

TO THE READER

If you have prayed this prayer, the publishers of GOD'S WARRIOR would like to hear from you. Please write your name on the coupon below, or if you don't want to cut up this book, just write on another sheet of paper, and mail it to:

> Indian Life Books
> P.O. Box 3765, RPO Redwood Centre
> Winnipeg, MB Canada R2W 3R6

- ❏ I prayed the prayer suggested in GOD'S WARRIOR, and now I would like more information on how to live as a Christian.

- ❏ Please send me some free literature on how to live as a Christian.

- ❏ Please write to me and tell me the name of someone who can give me personal help.

My name is _____

Address _____

Town _____

Prov/State _____ Postal/Zip _____

From the publishers of GOD'S WARRIOR...

More Good Reading

The Grieving Indian

by Arthur H. with George McPeek

This Canadian best seller is full of real-life stories about hurting people. Like GOD'S WARRIOR, it is also a book of encouragement, help and inspiration. Something every aboriginal should read. A must for everyone who works with Native people. Mass paperback 128 pages. $4.95 each (plus GST in Canada) plus postage.

Indian Life

Indian Life is North America's largest circulation Native publication. In its pages you will find positive news of Indian people and events, first-person stories, photo features, family life articles, and much more. Published six times a year. Write for a free sample copy. Find out why over 100,000 people read this paper. A one-year subscription is only $7.00 (plus GST in Canada). Quantity prices are available.

The Conquering Indian

The Conquering Indian is based on not just one person's life, but on those of seventy Native people; people whose lives have been dramatically changed because of their faith in Jesus Christ. The book tells the stories of how these people, young and old, reached out to Jesus and how He answered their pleas and helped them to have victory over the problems they faced. You, too, can face up to your problems and conquer them. This book can be used to guide you to the One who can help you win that victory. Mass paperback 332 pages. $6.95 each (plus GST in Canada) plus postage.

To order write to: Indian Life Ministries
PO Box 3765 RPO Redwood Centre
Winnipeg, MB R2W 3R6
Or phone: 1-800-665-9275

TO THE READER

If you have prayed this prayer, the publishers of GOD'S WARRIOR would like to hear from you. Please write your name on the coupon below, or if you don't want to cut up this book, just write on another sheet of paper, and mail it to:

Indian Life Books
P.O. Box 3765, RPO Redwood Centre
Winnipeg, MB Canada R2W 3R6

❏ I prayed the prayer suggested in GOD'S WARRIOR, and now I would like more information on how to live as a Christian.

❏ Please send me some free literature on how to live as a Christian.

❏ Please write to me and tell me the name of someone who can give me personal help.

My name is _____

Address _____

Town _____

Prov/State _____ Postal/Zip _____

From the publishers of GOD'S WARRIOR...

More Good Reading

The Grieving Indian

by Arthur H. with George McPeek

This Canadian best seller is full of real-life stories about hurting people. Like GOD'S WARRIOR, it is also a book of encouragement, help and inspiration. Something every aboriginal should read. A must for everyone who works with Native people. Mass paperback 128 pages. $4.95 each (plus GST in Canada) plus postage.

Indian Life

Indian Life is North America's largest circulation Native publication. In its pages you will find positive news of Indian people and events, first-person stories, photo features, family life articles, and much more. Published six times a year. Write for a free sample copy. Find out why over 100,000 people read this paper. A one-year subscription is only $7.00 (plus GST in Canada). Quantity prices are available.

The Conquering Indian

The Conquering Indian is based on not just one person's life, but on those of seventy Native people; people whose lives have been dramatically changed because of their faith in Jesus Christ. The book tells the stories of how these people, young and old, reached out to Jesus and how He answered their pleas and helped them to have victory over the problems they faced. You, too, can face up to your problems and conquer them. This book can be used to guide you to the One who can help you win that victory. Mass paperback 332 pages. $6.95 each (plus GST in Canada) plus postage.

To order write to: Indian Life Ministries
PO Box 3765 RPO Redwood Centre
Winnipeg, MB R2W 3R6
Or phone: 1-800-665-9275